Skipping Through Life

The Reason I Am

Sylvia McClain

Scribal Press
Detroit, Michigan

**Skipping Through Life, The Reason I Am
by Sylvia McClain**

Copyright © 2002 Sylvia McClain

Challenge Me With Motherhood and *The Lawn*, reprinted from University of Michigan-Dearborn Fall Lyceum 1997.

Layout and cover design
H. Buchanan-Gueringer, Aquarius Press

ISBN 0-9742643-2-6

Published by Scribal Press, Detroit, MI.

Printed in the United States of America

Contents

Acknowledgments

To Heather Buchanan-Gueringer, Sharon Stanford, Kimberley White, and Karen White-Owens: Thank you for your unwavering support of my desire to write these memories.

To Detroit Writer's Guild members who have believed in me from the beginning when I wasn't always sure myself, thank you.

To Marvin Arnett, everyone has a role model. In my quest to put it to words, you have been mine. As I watch you I am always reminded that it is never too late to turn one's dream into a reality.

To friends who didn't stop me from chasing my dream, thank you: you know who you are. To the others that worked with me to complete the task, thank you.

To my sister Judy, love does fuel the fire to conquer all. Love you much!

To my son, Momma believes in you, like you believed in Momma.

To my mother, I know you weren't always sure what I was doing but you stayed with me anyway.

Foreword

In this moving memoir, *Skipping Through Life*, Sylvia McClain relates her experiences as a young African American growing to maturity in a northern American City–Detroit, Michigan. The chapters are filled with human interactions that run the gamut from domestic violence, friendship, first love, and motherhood to the apex of her life–a near death experience. Sprinkled among these thought-provoking themes are chapters describing small, everyday occurrences that contain a wry humor that will literally make you laugh out loud. The sagas of the *New Teeth* and *The Lawn* are cases in point. This is memoir and urban social history at its best.

McClain narrates her experience with quiet dignity and faith. No matter how dire the circumstances, she manages to exhibit an optimism and strength of character that allows her to learn from the experience and use that knowledge to combat future problems. It is, however, the writer's ability to constantly reinvent herself during her growth toward an understanding of her own potential that is truly impressive.

Long after this book has left the reader's hands, the author's advice on how best to face troubled times will linger in the mind.

"Shift gears . . . and head in a new direction."
. . . And she did.

Marvin V. Arnett, Author
Pieces from Life's Crazy Quilt
(AMERICAN LIVES SERIES)
University of Nebraska Press

Introduction

For more decades than I need to count, I dreamed of being a writer. Not to write a book, just write. And for all the said decades I wrote. I would then lose the writing as I moved around. It was part of my process of growing up.

I had aspirations like most and I pursued them with unlimited enthusiasm. Yet, because I never knew why I wanted anything, I never really accomplished anything. One by one, I would set out to acquire this or acquire that. Always quitting before I got to whatever it was I sought.

One day, or more accurately stated, two weeks changed everything about me. Two weeks of solitude, quiet, and physical modifications took me to a higher plane. I was forced to examine myself. I had to look inward from the outside. Doing so, brought me face to face with the one true aspiration that dwelled in my heart. Love, not family love, love of friendships, or the love of a man but, self-love. Without knowing, for most of my young years all I wanted was to know selfhood. Having to contend with a new discovery, I began a quest to, piece by piece, construct a new me. The odd thing about it all was that, the new me was the old me I never knew.

That two-week hiatus opened a gateway to finding the girl and the woman I had lost. It wasn't an easy journey, not by a long shot. Therapy, spiritual enlightenment, and introspection were the costs I had to bear. But my crossover from self-deprecation to self-assurance carried a price I would pay ten fold if I had to make a choice again.

Over time I grew from a seedling to a full blossom. I became familiar with from whence I came to where I was headed. Sayings like "end to end," "full circle," and "alpha and the omega" were clear in my mind. The definitions of each were the results that I had achieved.

That is when I realized it was destiny that I write a book. Not a romantic's fantasy, but a book about life, the life I had evolved into. A book filled with the bits and pieces of molding, shaping, and nurturing that I endured to go from what I once was to what I am.

When I first heard Dr. Philip Graham talk about "defining moments," I smiled. You see, I was fully aware of what he meant. I had already at that time identified mine, hence, this book. Having already begun exploring those moments and putting them on paper, I knew then as I know now, the reason I am.

As you read this book, I hope you will experience what I have learned. Sometimes it is the big things, other times it's the little things and then for no explanation at all, some of those defining moments are what makes you who you are. They teach you acceptance, understanding, and then self-love.

To thine own self be true.

Daddy

While growing up, I thought two things of my father: hate and disgust. You heard me. I hated him because he was an alcoholic wife beater and child abuser. He disgusted me because he had talent, talent he didn't embrace. Without training he played guitar exquisitely. He was a master locksmith and when it came to cars, I seriously thought he was a genius. Yet, I hated him and he disgusted me, but he was my father.

My father and I didn't get along until much later in my life. The only reason we were ever able to tolerate each other was due to my getting tired of being angry with the world, my father included. When we did cross paths, we were cordial to each other, nothing else. It's when I stopped being angry that I began to see my father in a different light.

Although my father wasn't much of a father to me, my mother insisted his children treat him decently. We didn't have to like him but she ordered us to respect him. At the time I couldn't fathom what she saw in him that we didn't. He was nothing like the fathers of my friends. He definitely didn't compare with my Uncle Sam. Uncle Sam - religious, caring, the answer to my prayers - was my hero, not the man called my father. The five feet, eight-inches tall dark skin male of a small build was anything but admirable. Still, my mother insisted that we keep in mind he was the man who sired us.

I had no love for my father. All my memories growing up with him were nightmares. Once I found my mother in a pool of blood and another time my sister running hysterical around the house. I even had a dream one night of him chasing me down a dark alley clothed in a black cloak brandishing a sickle. No, there was no love for my father from me.

When I was seventeen, my father sent me to the corner party store to get him a pack of cigarettes. While I was there, a neighbor boy began teasing me. Ronald had a crush on me and every chance he got he drove me crazy. Well, the next thing I knew my father was standing on the opposite corner glaring at me. All the kids in the store began to pull away from me. They knew I was in trouble. Though I had not done anything wrong, they just knew. They knew my father and his ways. I hurried across the street and he asked me what I was doing.

"Nothing," I replied.

"Why were you taking so long?"

I don't remember what I said but I do remember the walloping smack he gave me upside my head. I was embarrassed, but I was more afraid of what was still to come. My father was peculiar. The more time he had to brew about how life treated him, the more violent he was. We started walking back to our house.

All the way home, my father spewed a tirade of insults toward me. Just as we passed the empty lot - four lots before ours - he swung his fist and "bam!" I was on the ground. There I lay face to face with the remnants of a metal post for a chain link fence. All I could think was *"What if I had landed a few more inches to my left?"* The remains of the post would be sticking out of the right side of my head. I would have died. Imagine my father almost killing me in cold blood. I could just see the 6:00 news. Cameras focused on a teenager, eyes wide open, with a round pole of metal pierced through her skull. At that time, as much as I was wishing it were a dream, it was all too real.

After we were home, I attended to my kitchen duties. As I washed the dinner dishes, I immersed my hands in the dishwater and massaged a butcher knife. Somewhere in my mind I had decided that enough was enough. I knew my father wasn't finished. He would dream up some wrongdoing I had done and come at me again. The butcher knife never left the dish pan.

True to form, my father came into the kitchen and picked up where he had left off. He threw question after question at me while never giving me a chance to answer one. Then out of the corner of my eye I saw him approaching closer. Instinctively I spun around and lunged the butcher knife toward my father's chest. I struck him once I know, maybe twice. However many times I struck his body, my father left the kitchen and said nothing more to me.

It was approximately when our scuffle ended my mother came in from work. My father started screaming at her about calling the police and an ambulance. He also expressed his belief that I was insane. He ordered her to get me out of his house. I don't recall the exact details afterwards of that summer night. Later in a courtroom, I vaguely remember the judge asking my mother if there was some place else I could live. Thank God my mom and her siblings were close. Just suffice it to say, I moved in with my Aunt Lillian and Uncle Sam. My nightmares didn't end. I worried about my mother and siblings, but things did quiet down for a long spell.

Later, as an adult, I began trying to piece the memories of my childhood together. When we grow up, we all wonder how we became what we turned out to be. I was puzzled most by the pieces that made up my father. As a child he influenced me more than even I knew at the time. With his wealth of talent I wondered what went wrong. You see my father was highly intelligent. Having only an eighth-grade education he served in the military and saw the world. He received many money bonuses as an employee of Ford Motor Company for innovative engineering ideas. He played guitar with famous musicians and was the only locksmith in Detroit who could open a timed lock without it blowing apart. My father was more than intelligent: he was creative. I began seeing my father in a new light. He had very few opportunities in life but he had many gifts. Raised during the years of much segregation and discrimination caused the lack of any opportunities to stifle his creative spirit. What I thought of him while growing up doesn't matter anymore. What I know now is, my father was the genesis of my artistic capabilities.

Thanks, Daddy.

Puberty

I was eleven years old, entering puberty and coming of age at the same time. "Gawk." In junior high there were cliques and sororities. It was the most important part of my life. How would I fit in? Well, needless to say, I became a member of a part nerdy and part cool bunch. If you can imagine that. The group consisted of four boys and two girls, one of them, me. We came together because we had classes together and a couple of us shared the same names. Hallelujah! We had something in common. The gang consisted of John, Gregory, Cornell B, Cornell J, Sylvia J, and Sylvia M. John, Gregory, Cornell B and Cornell J were best friends. Sylvia, who we called by her middle name Resia, and I just kind of gravitated toward each other and the boys. It was the beginning of a 37-year friendship between Resia and me.

Junior high in the 60's included the seventh,

eighth, and ninth grades. Those were truly the highlighted years of my life. I had the most memorable times in school then. I say this because I remember those years more than my senior high years. I had more fun in junior high.

The six of us helped each other with assignments, went to the movies together, and played jokes on each other. We were literally inseparable during and after school. The guys traded information about boys in return for information about girls. We obliged. Resia and I also had one other advantage hanging out with these guys. All of the guys were six feet tall and of massive builds. They were like big brother bodyguards.

Let me explain: once, a group of girls that everyone in the school were afraid of had passed the word that when school was over, Resia and I would get our butts kicked. Well, every student in the school planned to stay on the grounds to see the fight. They were not betting on us to win. Resia and I didn't see the guys that day, but we decided we wouldn't be intimidated by the bullies and met them after school.

At three o'clock the bell rang. As we left class, a whole crowd followed us to our lockers and to the exit door. Yep, there they were. Resia and I looked at each other, took a couple of deep breaths, locked hands and preceded down the stairs. As we were walking toward the bullies, out of nowhere appeared

John, Gregory, Cornell B, and Cornell J. The smiles on our faces spread from ear to ear. We knew everything would be ok. The guys joined us as we continued walking. The biggest girl stepped in front of us and pointed to Resia and said, "You. I want you." Another girl pointed to me and said, "And you're mine." It was at that moment that John confronted them and asked if they had a problem. Cornell J joined him while the other two guys stood beside Resia and me. A few exchanges of harsh words forced the bullies off to the side and away we went, all six of us. The guys laughed all the way to our homes as they teased Resia and me. But that was all right. They were our knights in shining armor. In your preteen years, having knights in shining armor were dreams come true.

Our three years at junior high were filled with moments of fun, seriousness, and anticipation. From each other we learned patience, acceptance, and gratitude. We grew up together. The six of us became so popular, and others wanted to join us in the fun. We let them, but they would never accomplish what we had, three very special years of friendship and love.

Resia and I talk now sometimes about those years. We wonder whatever happened to everyone. We lost contact because the boys went to different senior highs. It's funny how you remember the oddest times in your life.

Thirty-eight years later, I still think about all the people from junior high. The ones I liked and the ones that made me want to puke. I did run into one boy from those days and he's now a doctor. He always had a crush on me. I wonder if he still does. "Dr. Herbert and Mrs. Sylvia Washington" has a very good ring to it.

First Love

When you're a fourteen-year-old girl, you're not sure if you like boys or not. What you do know is that they will eventually be a part of your life. My life took a turn when I became involved with a boy who was three years older than me and one half of a matched pair. With him I learned to develop healthy relationships with men. It was always easier for me to be friends, not lovers, with them. All because one half of that matched pair was my first love, my first lover and my first friend of male persuasion.

The twins were every girl's heartthrobs. They were six feet in height, had hazel eyes, played great basketball, had cars of their own, and could speak lines that made females young and old melt like butter after hearing them. Call it double pleasure to a pubescent girl. Most girls could not tell them apart. It was no problem whatsoever for me. Dionel had a mole on his cheek under his left eye. Lionel did not.

That seems simple enough but they were really different people who happen to look to most exactly alike.

When Dino first took me out, I had been warned that I would not be able to handle his charming manner, his smooth method of operation or the wisdom that came with his age. He was seventeen. Surprisingly, he was nothing like I had been told he would be. Dino introduced himself to my mother when he picked me up and held a ten minute conversation with her which included a promise to have me home by curfew. My head started spinning in low gear. He was more than charming. He was fabulous.

I remember very little more about that first date. What I do remember is what I learned while I was Dino's girlfriend. Dino and I spent a lot of time getting to know each other. We talked a lot sharing our dreams and fantasies. He wanted the world and I wanted just to be with him. Ok, ok, I wanted more than that, but when you're fourteen and you're swooning in the aura of the catch of the year, you don't think much about your life's upcoming plans. Leave it to say I was so enthralled by him and his engaging smile and patience that I could barely keep my mind on keeping the other girls at bay, let alone what I was going to do with my life.

Yet, Dino became a new age teacher for me.

Through him I was introduced to the meaning of education, success, having money and sexual feelings. He explained the difference between desires and needs. Although he was just a seventeen-year-old child, I felt he knew more than someone 50 years of age. I truly believed that he had been here before and was sent back to mentor me. He had reminded me most of my Uncle Sam. My uncle was a loving husband, hard worker, very spiritual and shared everything he had and knew with others. That is what Dino did for me.

I remember Dino because he made me accept becoming a woman. Yes, I was only fourteen at the time but, he knew I wasn't going to stay fourteen forever. This is when my lessons began. Little by little, he held conversations with me on how I should portray myself to the world. Although my mother had talks with me about being a lady, Dino discussed being a woman. There is a difference. To my new found friend I was to simulate Madame C.J. Walker, Mary McCleod Bethune, and Shirley Chisholm all rolled into one. I was to value myself like no other would or could. No matter what others preached or advertised, I was never to forget that I was going to become a woman of stature, bestowed with much pride, dignity, and common sense.

It was the common sense while growing up, which he elaborated on the most. Dino wanted most for me to realize that as a young attractive girl, I would be approached by many guys with more than my best interest on their minds. That I would appear to be gullible to the ways of men and only I could send messages that dispelled any notions of seduction, eroticism, and debauchery. The conversations we held on these matters gave me insight to the male psyche. Why did he hold them? Who knows? I just thank him for them. Because of the talks, I grew up with a definite set of criteria. One: I am precious. Therefore never think that I can be talked to, talked at, or talked about without respect. Two: My body is my temple. In my body temple, I celebrated me at the altar. Three: Knowledge is and always will be power. In my own time I will make up my own mind. Dino taught me what loving me was all about. Being fed this much information by a seventeen-year-old boy was more than a mouthful. I was stuffed.

Over the year that Dino was my boyfriend, I matured faster than what was ever expected. I graduated from junior high school, got a full time job at the Wayne State University library, and started planning my life's vocation. Dino and I kept in touch now and then. But he drifted into a lifestyle that I wanted no part of, drugs, criminal activities, and fast living. Everything he had warned me against. Then one day it was over. Yet I thought of him a lot and thanked him even more in my heart. I had become a woman.

The woman I became learned that you didn't have to make deals you didn't like. You didn't have to sell yourself short. You didn't have to give up anything you didn't want to give. That the only thing you had to do was, stay true to yourself. In this way I grew and flourished.

One last thing. When I met Dionel, I was virtuous. When we split up, I had found the true meaning of knowing and being in love, as well as the meaning of consent. To Dionel, all my love forever.

Challenge Me with Motherhood

If you survive the job of motherhood for at least eighteen years, you can govern the world. Trust me, I know. I'm a mother. Twenty years ago, I became a mother and I survived. So did my son, Rasheen. Now let me tell you, survival was no guarantee—for him or I. Day one, Rasheen came into this world with an attitude. He would not tolerate any newfangled formulas or disposable diapers. Born allergic to all modern time-savers, his little body insisted: "You will feed me the old-fashioned way, Pet milk and Karo syrup, and use cloth diapers, the kind you must wash." I just knew he planned this in the womb. This was my introduction into motherhood.

In his first year on this Earth, Rasheen challenged himself and I. He started with a cut lip — two stitches required —at six months when he attempted to walk around a cocktail table. He moved on to more ambitious activities, like a busted skull about three or four times. A visit to the emergency ward became such a ritual that I no longer had to check in at the hospital. We had a reserved room. Our visits were so routine that one doctor asked me if I were doing this on purpose. Need I tell you what I said to her? No one had explained to me that it was natural for a child his age to climb windows, bathroom sinks, and kitchen counters. In the mean time, discovering he had asthma also contributed to our residency at the hospital emergency room. He hadn't even reached the age of one yet, and it was taking its toll on me.

The second year wasn't much better. At fourteen months he decided that life was not interesting enough for me, so he chose to have a seizure while suffering from a cold and an elevated temperature; hence, a call to 911 and an overnight stay at the hospital. Then, if that wasn't enough, in the emergency room he chose to be uncooperative in giving blood and bathed the staff of one technician, two nurses, and one doctor in the bright red liquid. Being a hysterical mother I wasn't much help, but I had to hold him to obtain a blood sample. Wait! That's not the end. Admitted for a short stay and ensconced in his hospital room, my son decided to disconnect every IV connection to his body and pull the oxygen tent down. If you think he was a handful for the hospital staff, remember, I had to live with him every day. I was seriously reconsidering this motherhood thing.

I often consulted my own mother on how to make life easier for my son and I. She would just say, "What do you think I went through with you and your brothers and sisters." I would start to cry as I realized I wasn't going to see my son's adulthood. He had to be trying to commit suicide. I know he was only eighteen months old, but he knew what he was doing.

The first summer Rasheen was really able to enjoy started the new trend of exploration my son seemed to delight in. He discovered my younger brother's skateboard. I can only guess that my son, forgot he was a baby. He mounted the skateboard and, this time, a trip to the emergency and the hospital dental ward ensued. It didn't matter that he had just lost his two front teeth — that's the price you pay when you play. He was eighteen months old and there was no end in sight. This was getting to be a bit much. I was a single parent, you see, before it was fashionable.

Over the next three years, Rasheen tested my endurance by way of nail polish remover, house paint, and automobiles. All of this before he started school at five. Drinking polish remover, redecorating the house and learning to drive at the age of four were all the things my son had decided he needed to know how to do.

Somehow, he eventually made it to maturity. He went to school and became normal. Of course, he got into your usual mischief from kindergarten to twelfth grade. He made excuses for not doing homework, he searched for his place in life, and he went through the rebellious stage of the teen years. Yet, he made it and so did I. What does all this mean? Surviving your child's formative years gives you credentials to run the world.

I know, I'm a mother.

Have You Seen My Sister?

My sister never had a chance. She had to grow up wading through life when life was an ocean. I watched her miss out somehow on a light to guide her. No one taught her pride, dignity, respect, or self esteem. So she learned it the only way she knew how. She took to the streets. She dropped out of school at sixteen, hooked up with an older man, became a single parent at eighteen and five years down the line joined the Sniffers Club. It all happened so fast we never saw it coming.

I'm the oldest of five, in a typical urban Black family. My father worked in an auto plant and my mother was a housewife. Mom took us to church every Sunday. Daddy played the guitar for several different bands most weekends. He played the blues and without knowing it, one of us was bound to live it.

This sister I'm speaking of was the second

born. During her early years everything she did or didn't do, was compared with her siblings and their actions. I know that's where it all started. I know my parents meant well, but they just didn't know any better. That's the thing about raising kids. They don't come with instruction manuals when they're born, but you already know that.

Unlike the rest of us, they dealt my sister a lousy hand when she was born. She was very fair in skin color, having no interest in school and craving attention. Put yourself in her place: your four brothers and sisters are darker in skin tone, do quite well in school and are the quiet types. Talk about being the black sheep in a herd of white wool! Anyway, she had her hands full of crap and she wasn't given an instruction manual either. She was to fit in when there was no space available.

In 1982 after a long lay off from an auto manufacturer my sister had to move in with me. With two kids in tow, my sister slowly began her descent. Five months - little by little - my eyes were opened to my sister's addiction. First was the never-ending cold she always had. She sniffed continuously. Morning, noon, or night, it didn't matter. She just couldn't get rid of that cold. After finding a job that paid her "under the table," she was always broke. Although she was collecting unemployment, getting paid for work on the side and getting money from a new boyfriend, my sister said she couldn't afford half of the $350.00 it cost to run our home. Can you believe with steady funds she couldn't afford $175.00? Hell, I was working two jobs at the time and still brought home less than her.

One day I added things up and the balance didn't come out right. There were too many unexplained things. She slept all day, she was eating us all out of house and home, she stayed out all night when she got off work at 2:00 A.M. Something was definitely not right. I confronted her and she chose to move out instead of facing the situation. It was at this time my family and I found out she had become hooked three years earlier. My sister snorted cocaine and she was a bonafide addict.

Over the next five years my sister's life became a roller coaster ride. She and the kids lived in more places than one could name. Some of them were good but most of them were rat holes. One year my sister moved so many times that the kids were enrolled in ten different schools. Keep in mind a school year is from September to June. Ten months, ten moves and they still had no home.

My mother, another sibling, and I tried hard to help my sister. We got her to confess to her addiction. We helped her get into rehabilitation programs. My mother and I even took custody of the kids at different times. Yet, nothing seemed to help. My sister was in denial. She still is. Oh we heard all the excuses. "Ya'll just don't understand what I'm going through," she said. "I can't help myself. Everybody is against me." Yep, we heard them all. So did counselors, doctors, old friends, extended family members, neighbors, you name them. Everyone heard her. The problem was she didn't hear herself. Escaping was easier for her than to stand up and fight. But that's what drug addicts do.

In the new millennium, my sister, alive and still hooked, has lived in her fantasy world for 25 years. You would think that she would be tired. I know I am. I'm tired of catching newscasts about unidentified dead women. I'm tired of reading about shootouts between drug lords in drug houses. I'm tired of neighborhood talks about so and so looking so bad. I'd like to put it to rest, but I can't. She's my sister. I don't like her. I love her.

So now and then I sit around thinking about "back in the day," because I wonder what she's doing now. The little things cross my mind. You know... *where is she, who is she with and what is she doing?*

Have you seen my sister?

Before . . .

It was November of 1983. I was gliding across the stage at the most prominent supper club in the city. In one week there was going to be a fashion show, the show of shows in Black society. A promotion by *Bosom Buddies* and I was a Bosom Buddies star.

Then it started: a little nagging pain at the edge of my left eyebrow. I took a couple of aspirin and continued through the rehearsal. It was about 10 o'clock Sunday morning, the Sunday before Thanksgiving. The rehearsal lasted four hours and so did the ache in my head. In fact, the ache became a whopper despite my having taken several aspirins. I went home, drank some tea, took a few more painkillers and began to feel very strange. Call it a hunch but, somehow I knew something wasn't quite right. My head still ached consistently after six hours.

I had a perfume home party to do that evening. A friend of my mother had agreed to host it. Phoning my mother to express some trepidation, I told her I'd come by and explain why when I got there. I also asked her, as an afterthought, to come and look for me if I did not arrive within fifteen minutes. I lived only one mile from my mother: call it another hunch.

As I prepared for the home party, I couldn't stop thinking, *"I must get to my mother's house."* Repeatedly I felt an endless need to be with my mother. In a hurry I left home and headed to 1963 Richton Street. I had to get there as soon as possible.

When I arrived at my Mom's, she looked at me and said, "What's wrong? You look like you're in pain."

"I am Momma and I'm scared." To my mother I explained what had occurred while I was at the rehearsal. She suggested I try another kind of pain remedy and lie down a while. I took her advice and approximately thirty minutes later, arose crying and told my mother that the pain was unbearable. "I think I better get to a hospital."

When I opened my eyes, I knew where I was. Relieved, I knew that my intuition of being cared for by my mother had been true. She was at my bedside when I awakened. Momma tried to explain what had happened. Understanding how I had been asleep for two weeks was difficult for me. What I felt then was that I had a good night's rest. I requested the doctor's appearance.

Little did I know my life had changed. In two short weeks, of which I could not remember, I had faced death. Not once, not twice, but three separate times. There had definitely been some modification in me.

After being informed of the bubble in my head and the options I had, it dawned on me I wasn't ready to say good-bye. Yet, I wasn't ready to take chances either. I was left with only one choice. The knife. If I didn't believe in the knife I would most assuredly have to say so long but, if I trusted the knife . . . , a fifty-fifty chance was better than no chance at all. I signed the forms, closed my eyes, and prayed. Oh, how I prayed.

. . . and After

I was elated the next time I opened my eyes. Everything I saw, the four blue walls, other people walking by, needles in my arms, were all real. It wasn't a dream and not an afterlife experience. I had beat the odds. Nevertheless, I felt different. I felt a void and had one question, *why me*? After being forced to decide, I couldn't remember things. So much was left unspoken and I was still young.

Confusion, shock and anger became my reaction. They became the words that described me well. I was confused; my thoughts were scattered.

Traumatized, I was repeatedly indignant. I wanted an explanation for what I had gone through. Surely, there was a scientific interpretation but not an emotional one. With only that to go on, I pitched fits. To me it was all so unfair. Having committed no crime - moral or illegal - life was treating me unjustly.

Before I was released from the hospital, they put me through physical dissection, emotional chaos, and psychological analyses. My unanswered question was still *Why me*? Yet, on paper I was deemed sound with a recommendation of therapy attached. This is what I took home when I was discharged.

For the first two to three weeks I found myself in a haze. Although I was happy that I was alive, I could tell that something was amiss. Nothing was as it should be. It wasn't chaotic but, it wasn't normal either. I first noticed my inability to remember how to vocalize simple words, words like, "the," "me," and "what," the common words used in everyday speech. I would open my mouth and they were lost in the transmission from my brain to my corresponding oral body part. After that, I realized I could remember specific accounts of the 60's but not things that occurred just days before. At the hospital the psychiatrist had said I may suffer some memory loss for a short time. Still, to me, losses of memory in any duration frightened me. Hadn't I suffered enough when I lost all knowledge of existence for two weeks? What if the doctor had been wrong and my memory would never be recaptured? Without detecting it, the questions I had, bred anger within my psyche.

So distraught, I wanted to understand why my life had seen so many catastrophes. This health issue was the last of that which I felt I could handle anymore. What was wrong with me? Didn't I do everything right? I was raising my son as best I could as a single parent. I held a good job and was connected spiritually, or so I thought. So why was I being sentenced to death? For a year I attempted to shut down my inquisitive mind. Returning to work, moving to a new abode, and finding part time work to supplement my regular income, in my head I was moving forward. Things were going to be better. My life began soaring upward. Suddenly I broke down.

For three days I sat in a corner of my apartment and cried. I didn't call in to work and I didn't answer the phone. My son came home after school and became the guardian to his mother. At eleven years of age, he fixed his own meals, cleaned the apartment, and comforted his mother. "It's going to be ok Momma," I remember him saying. What he didn't know was that his mother was sick. Not physically, but mentally distressed. He couldn't possibly know, when even I had no idea I was ill.

The department head I worked under was a caring individual. Thank God. He contacted my mother and encouraged her to go and check on me. He felt something was askew. It wasn't like me not to report to work nor respond to phone calls at home. Three days of it caused him to be concerned. My mother came to my apartment and found me all messed up. After helping me with a bath and getting me to bed, my mother suggested that maybe I truly needed therapy. She offered logical explanations why a professional could help me sort things out in my head. I finally agreed. I set up my first appointment the next day and begun what was going to be six months of one hour biweekly sessions.

Over this period a female psychiatrist helped me to open up and talk about the things that bothered me. My childhood, my social life, single-parenthood, employment, school, money, owning a home, marriage, everything any individual would have to deal with as part of life. In doing so, she and I found that I was full of anger. Angry that I was a single parent, had not finished the schooling I desired, didn't own property, wasn't in an intimate relationship, and struggling financially. As far as I was concerned, life had cheated me out of happiness and someone else was supposed to pay, not me.

There was no defining moment but, at my last session I suddenly realized I didn't want to continue living as I had been, visiting with a doctor and getting nowhere, with continuous inquiries into *"Why me?"* and conversations about the past that could not be undone. I wanted out. It was time, time for me to take stock of myself and change me. As the last session came to a close, I thanked the doctor and explained I would not be coming back. You see, I had suddenly accepted the fact that the anger I embraced was the very apparatus that was draining me of my life. For years I had repeatedly worshiped the very device that dug the hole in which I wallowed, a hole of self loathing. I didn't love me because I never liked me, and why not? Because I never knew who I was or what I ever wanted to be. All of this in the name of fear. I wanted to live with all my heart but I was afraid to open it. I wanted to experience all I could but not be exposed. After thirty years of living, nothing had ever prepared me for death. I literally had to die in order to learn to live.

The trip to recapture "me" began. I started listening to my voice. It asked me to get ready to let go and let in, to drop everything I clung to and to reach out for all that I could have. I was to cleanse myself in stages of destructive thoughts and restore my spirit, the spirit I once had but lost. Suddenly, a prayer I remembered from childhood took hold of me. The Serenity Prayer. Over and over, three lines rang in my head: "Change the things you can, accept the things you can't, but have the wisdom to know the difference between the two." Without realizing it I was about to be reborn, and over time that is exactly what happened. It was a struggle but I did it. I reshaped my life. By the time the decade of the 90's was approaching, I was a different person. I had grown into a stronger being because I had discovered the source of my strength, the force within me and its power to create. Now I face obstacles with new resolve. If I can change it, I do. If I can't, I accept, and I'm never confused about which is which.

The Personal Ads

It all started after I became seriously ill one year and awoke from an unconscious state in a hospital. Thirty years old and I had almost died. The first things I thought of all started with "If I could have, would have, should have." I could have written a book by now. Why hadn't I traveled around the world yet? At thirty I should be married. Well, it was time to get busy.

The writing of a book was going to take some time and a trip around the world would take money. Neither of them, I felt, was within immediate reach. So I started with the easy one. Marriage. How hard could it be getting married? Now I know you're all thinking, "Ump!" Still, look at my options. I was not exactly an established author and money didn't grow on a tree in my backyard. Finding a suitable mate looked more like the first step to take. No more "If I could have, would have, and should haves." I was going to do it, just in case I found myself in another health crisis.

I had already tried all the usual routes: church activities, introductions through friends, supermarkets, nightclubs, blind dates, on-the-job social affairs, my best friend's cousin, a neighborhood block party, even my sister's boyfriend's brother. Tried them all I did. What was left? Aha, the *"personal ads."* My last port of call, "Stop the ship, I'm getting off."

So where do I start? Should I answer the newspaper ads? Should the ad come from *"Speaking from the Heart"* or *"Romance Connection?"* What about using videos? I opted for the written ads. It cost me no more than the price of a postage stamp, although it was going to take more work than I thought. As I compared the different papers, I found I would have to go back to school. Getting a degree in abbreviations was like pursuing a degree in teenage slang. Neither was a picnic.

First, I had to master the single letters. "B" is for black, "W" is for white, "C" is for Christian. Get my drift? Then I advanced to second level classes, where I had to learn combinations: DM w/c or SJM. Now this was important. I needed to know if the man had children and what religion he practiced. How could I meet a man without knowing the statistics of his life? At the third level I was introduced to the personal ad dialect. For example: "habitless" equals don't smoke or drink and "clean" equals no sexually transmitted diseases. They are not your usual dictionary definitions. "Hey, let's just start with a date!"

Then the examinations began. My first encounter brought me in contact with someone who didn't even have a car. Ok, Ok, no problem, I could pick him up. Next time, remind me to response to an ad with "Do you have any wheels?" He was really a nice guy, but, he had no ambition, was low on funds, and was not a romantic. So I'm a little picky. What can I say? The second rendezvous, bad-d-d neighborhood, no funds, I repeat *no funds*, and an assortment of problems I can't begin to recount. What the heck, I tried it again. My third meeting brought me face to face with the most perfect man I had ever met. Gainfully employed, generous, caring, and an active Christian. So what's the problem? No chemistry. Are you surprised? I wasn't. I have to feel something, magic sunsets and symphonic music aren't required but something is. A few chuckles, a few tears, a little ego stroking wouldn't hurt. Alas, the search through the personal ads didn't seem to be working out.

On and on this went for about eight years. Did I find an appropriate mate? No. But I'm still waiting. I keep looking while I'm pursuing the status of author and planning trips as much as possible. Did I give up on the personal ads? Na. I just scan them now and then. If I see one that peaks my interest, I respond. I have met some interesting people and made a few new friends. "Hold that ship I want to get on," is my rallying call now. Like most women, I'll probably meet a dream mate when I stop looking for him.

Forgotten Birthdays

Every year I sit by the phone waiting for that elusive call. I start to feel something in my chest beat fast while I wait for that once-in-a-lifetime surprise to surface and that I can treasure forever. I even look for the most fantastic gift to appear. Yet as I start to experience the early pains, I justify the reasons for them. I tell myself that there's been an unexpected delay and everything will be all right, just wait and see.

Nevertheless, it happens anyway. First the right ventricle of my heart breaks, then the left. The pain increases and I start looking for a way to ignore it. I tell myself I have things to do. I don't have time to sit around with idle hands and an idle mind. It's not healthy. But, I can't help but wonder, is it me? What did I do wrong? Doesn't anybody care?

Then comes the completely broken heart. Not from the ones we think we will grow old with or from the family we think is perfect, but from friends, many friends. The ones I've known for more than 30 years. Some friends I grew up with and some I met and developed our relationships through work and other activities. We've been friends for a very long time and I feel that we know each other like that classic book everyone had to read in school. Then it happens. They break my heart. When I crossed the bridge to the so called guaranteed maturity of the 40's, no one called, sent a card or surprised me.

Now this may sound trivial to some people, but this is a major deal with me. In a year of 365 days there are only two that mean the world to me. One, Mothers Day, because I am a mother and two, my birthday, because it's just that, my birthday. I realize that I was not the only person born on that day in that year but, how many others do my friends know? My friends are supposed to know me. Now, either I don't completely understand the meaning of friends or they do know me and just don't care, is what I felt the day I turned 40. My friends not caring, people who shared intimate secrets, who are part of a sisterhood, who are comrades against the odds, not caring? Impossible! So the question became, why did they break my heart?

After five days passed I had only heard from one friend. She called the very next day and apologized for forgetting. She's forgiven. Where were the others? Forgiving would soothe an aching heart. I did so want to forgive. To live without friends is like being without bread and water, death of substance and soul. They are still my friends, aren't they?

Who can explain why some of us break hearts, not me? It brings tears, it generates anger, and it hurts, and that's the thing that bothers me the most. It hurts. There's no medicine to stop the ache, there's no cure for the illness, and only time heals the pain. Time seems to take forever too. Waiting for time so you can forgive leaves one with the feeling of eternity going by. Still, you have no choice but to be patience. Friends are a part of being complete. To function without them is impossible. I just knew they would come through eventually and as always I would forgive them. That's what friends do.

The Lawn

It was the first weekend after the last frost. I'd spent the winter boning up on all the information I could to turn my lawn into the most exquisitely manicured lawn in the neighborhood.

I awoke about 6:30 A.M. I put on some old jeans and a heavy T-shirt, dug out a pair of worn out shoes and socks, and headed to the large backyard. With a rake in my hand, I proceeded to gather debris from the winter. I suddenly noticed that the spring sprouts of grass looked like moss — the moss that grows along the base of a tree. I kneeled down to get a closer look and lo and behold it just rolled away. A wave of fear came over me. Me, the suit wearing, briefcase toting, corporate woman may not know a lot about lawns, but I know trouble in the yard when I see it. Grass doesn't just roll away like a rug. I stroked the lawn a couple of times with the rake and they appeared. I went flying into the house, woke my son, Rasheen, and ordered him to get dressed. "There's something I want you to look at in the yard." He hemmed and hawed, but I was insistent.

When we returned to the yard, I used a rake to turn over some dirt. This time there were what looked to me like an army of bugs. I said to my son, "Look! What are those things?" He replied, "Uh-oh, we got 'em. They're the little white worm things with brown booties."

"Say what?"

"I think they call 'em grubs." My head started spinning. What the hell are grubs? Where did they come from? How do I get rid of them? Why me?

It was at this time I decided professional help was needed. I said to my son, "Kill one of them and put it in something I can take with me. I'm going to go to the hardware store for help." So he did and off I went.

As I crossed the portal into what had become the "grub center," I discovered that I was not alone in the world of panic. Before me stood men and women with a look of anguish on their faces. I proceeded first to the corner of the store that housed the famous "Ortho" problem solver book of knowledge on lawn care and all the other lawn care materials. I checked the index, then flipped to the section on grubs. It was after reading how I would need chemicals I couldn't even pronounce, I closed the book and said, "Sir, excuse me. Could you assist me? Is this a grub?" as I shoved my hand before him.

"Sure, how can I help you?"

"What do I do?" I asked in frustration. He began to inform me of how to get rid of the pest first, then how I would have to reseed the lawn, water it, fertilize it, and prepare it for the next wave of beetles. Japanese beetles. The grubs were their babies and they would grow up and become mothers. Get the picture? When I returned home, I had two bags of Diazinon granules, a three pound box of grass seed, a bow rake, and determination. I was also $40 poorer. "No problem," I said to myself, "I'm going to whip this." Three simple steps is all it would take. First, to eliminate the little things, I must first turn the dirt over to expose the grubs. Next I had to sprinkle the dirt with the Diazinon granules and smooth the dirt out, then water a little and wait fourteen days. No problem. I grabbed my shovel and began.

Thirty minutes later, sweating and aching, I looked at my yard and sighed. I live on what is called a double lot — picture enough land to build two houses on. I was going nowhere fast. Then it hit me. If it's going to take a while, I'd better start in the front of the house. It's the part of my property everyone in the whole world can see. My God, what would they think? Here's this house on the corner surrounded with beautiful potted plants and it has no lawn.

It was 10:00 A.M. and three hours into the morning. I had accomplished nothing. The front yard had more grubs than the back. This was serious business. I started over again with step one. Ten minutes into my mission, my son appeared at the front door.

"What are you doing mom?" There I was bending over trying to turn dirt over with a shovel and he asked me such a simple question.

"What does it look like?" I retorted. At this time he came out the door, walked over to me and said, "Let me show you how to do it." He took the shovel from my hand, placed the bottom edge on the dirt, put one foot on the top edge and pushed. Up came the dirt and to the side he tossed it. After doing it a couple of times, he handed the shovel to me and said, "See?" How was I supposed to know you didn't have to break your back when using a shovel? From this point on, it was smooth sailing. One hour later, my front yard against the house and next to the curb was spread with the granules and the elimination process had begun. All I had to do now was wait fourteen days to put down the grass seed, and fourteen days after that, my lawn would be back to normal.

The two weeks came. I had missed the first

fertilizing date. Pat Wooley - my new guidance counselor at the hardware store - assured me it was ok. "No harm done. You can mix grass seed with the fertilizer when it's time to spread it." It was time. I brought the box of grass seed out of the garage, stuck my hand in, grabbed a handful, and commenced to sprinkle the seed on the dirt. In approximately one minute, I knew that sprinkling with my hand was not going to work. I couldn't do all of it by hand. Off to the "grub center" I went again to pick up the tool to help me make it through step two.

Pouring the grass seed and fertilizer into my new EZ handspreader, I began spreading the dirt. Step three was to level the soil so that the new sprouts would grow and produce an even lawn. Here is where trouble reappeared. Pat, my counselor, had said all I needed was a bow rake. I had bought one. It wasn't doing the job. I would rake in one direction and the dirt would move in another. The dirt was not becoming level. I tried patting the dirt down with a shovel. It did the job, but it worked only on two square feet at a time, the size of the shovel. At this time a neighbor came over and asked me why I didn't use a lawn roller. As politely as I could, I informed him I didn't have money to buy one, nor the money to rent one. He stood there for a minute looking from one side of my lawn's edge to the other and said, "Use your car. You got a driveway on each side of the lawn, drive over it." I looked from side to side and thought, that'll work. I went inside to get my sister and explained the situation. I got in my car and began driving back and forth across my front lawn while my sister playing airport marshaller.

The next fourteen days I watered the dirt a little everyday. I shooed small children off of the dirt, sprayed the birds and dogs with water and finally my grass returned. With it came pests, other bugs, and weeds. However, I handled them with appropriate means and succeeded in producing a richly colored lawn, but only in the front.

I never did get around to the backyard. It took about two months to finish the front. About this time it was the middle of summer, time for a family reunion, and I hadn't even begun having summer fun. I figured knowing what I know now — like covering the dirt with hay to guard against the birds eating the seeds, and roping off the lawn against the children and dogs — the backyard would be a cinch next spring. Besides, Pat said, "Some of the beetles lay their eggs in early fall. They don't hatch again until spring." That's alright with me. I may be $60 poorer, but I'm wiser. A few dollars more and I'll pay someone else to do the job.

New Teeth

It was Saturday, my day off from work and as usual I had things to do, places to go, stuff to pick up. By eleven thirty that morning and I had already motored my car to the farmer's market, the cleaners, the hardware store, Office Depot and found myself standing in the middle of a strip mall. Two and a half hours to go before I was to be at a meeting. A ga-zillion things still on my agenda and I was hungry. I hadn't had any breakfast - not even a cup of tea. Having brunch sounded good.

I looked at my watch and thought, I've got time. Besides my stomach told me I'd better make time before it turned on me. Off to the food court I went. Checking out my food choices, I opted for Chinese, fried rice and an eggroll, something simple and quick to eat. I could still eat, pickup some hosiery and get to the meeting. No one told me that fake teeth would be my downfall.

First let me explain, I'm referring to teeth I was not born with. I bought them from a distributor through the retailer we all call our dentist. It is a silver band with five off-white teeth attached to pink plastic. It's a partial. Partials and rice don't mix. Why? Those little kernels of grain have a way of sliding under a metal band and driving one crazy. So I took them out of my mouth. Placed it on the tray and enjoyed my simple meal.

Approximately fifteen minutes later, the grumbling subsided in my belly. In a nearby trash barrel I dumped the paper refuse. Just as I was about to go on my way, I froze. I immediately realized that along with the leftover rice and eggroll in the barrel were my teeth. I was suddenly alarmed. "Oh my God. What have I done?" Five hundred dollars mixed with the trash. I didn't have five hundred dollars to throw away. I had to get my teeth back.

I took a deep breath and began picking through the garbage. On bended knees, using only my thumb and first finger, I started removing the garbage bit by bit. A few minutes later half the barrel was on the floor and mall patrons were thinking I was probably missing a few marbles upstairs. You see I was dressed pretty stylish. An ankle length blue skirt with a red sweater and print scarf around my neck. My blue riding boots even matched. The coat and gloves I carried were designer brands. Outwardly

I looked to be a woman of good stock, and I was rummaging through the garbage. You get the picture?

I stood up and looked around for assistance. A guy with the maintenance crew appeared at the other side of the food court and I motioned for him to come to me. He obliged. I explained my dilemma and asked if he would yellow tape the area off and advise patrons not to be alarmed. He had a sympathetic look about him and brought another barrel to me. He showed me how I could take things from one barrel, drop them in the second barrel and not make a big mess. It made good sense to me because I had already made a mess on the floor. The young man said he would help me but I insisted that I could handle it alone.

Fifteen minutes passed and I was reaching the bottom with no teeth in sight. Now I was really ready to panic. "Where did my teeth go? I couldn't leave without them." I felt there had to be another way to solve this problem. The guy came back and asked, "Any luck?" I must have had the look of a sick puppy on my face because he offered another solution.

"Why don't I take the barrel out back to the dumpster and pour it out?" he asked. "You'll have more room to look through the stack and maybe you'll find your teeth."

"I'll try anything. You go ahead and I'll be right behind you."

Trying to pull myself together as any dignified woman would, I got up off the floor, straightened my clothes, lifted my head high and proceeded to the alley. As I approached the area of dumpsters, all I saw was half-eaten food, candy wrappers and only God knew what else. I thought, "I've got to stick my hands in that mess." Oh well, here goes nothing.

The gentleman helped me by literally doing what he said he would. He poured all the garbage onto the concrete. I took a seat next to the pile and began picking through the garbage. One by one, piece by piece, I began searching for my teeth. After another fifteen minutes went by, I was down to the last two pieces of garbage and still no teeth in sight. I was about to cry. How was I going to speak at the meeting? In my head I could just hear myself saying, "Hello, my name is Sifia MaCain" in front of a room of strangers. My partial was only three months old. I didn't want to sound like Daffy Duck with a mouth full of saliva.

Then I saw a glint of light. Two pieces of trash left and something was shining. Yes! Thank God metal reflects light. I was saved! I lifted the partial and froze, again. Think about this. I had just retrieved my teeth from the bottom of about 100 lbs. of garbage. I couldn't possibly just stick that thing back into my mouth. Like magic, the guy from maintenance appeared again. "Did you find them?"

"Yes. Would you by any chance have any toothpaste I could use?"

"Sure, in the locker room the crew uses. Follow me." I was astonished. I had not really expected him to give me an affirmative, but you never know.

In the locker room, I took another gamble. "Would you also have a toothbrush I could use?" Now this is where it got really good. He not only had a toothbrush I could use but, a toothbrush in an unopened, sealed wrapper. He handed it to me and said to toss it in the trash when I finished. I suddenly started thinking, were toothbrushes part of the maintenance crew's benefits or were they perks? We all know benefits and perks are not the same in business. Anyway, I cleaned my partial and put them back where they belonged, inside my mouth. I looked at my watch and realized I had just enough time to get to the meeting. If I didn't catch many red traffic lights, no one would be the wiser about what I had just gone through.

As I was driving, I began to recant in my head what had just happen. That's when I burst out laughing. I laughed so hard I had to pull off to the side of a major highway. The road I was traveling was not an expressway, but no one traveled less than 50 miles per hour on it. Talking about laughing till you cry. The tears poured out faster than a waterfall.

No way could I keep up with traffic conditions when I couldn't see straight. I was an accident about to happen. Think back a moment. I must have looked hilarious in the mall. People probably thought I was a well dressed bag lady rummaging for food. I couldn't stop laughing.

Then a police officer appeared. Wearing a spotless uniform and looking worried, he approached my car. With a courteous demeanor he asked if I was OK. He had to have thought I was in some traumatic state. What did I do? I laughed even harder. How was I going to explain to the police officer what was wrong? "Oh officer, don't mind me, I'm just laughing at myself. You should have seen me in the mall digging in garbage for my teeth." Yeah, right. I found enough composure from within to explain my laughter. He looked at me like I was crazy and advised me to move on.

After I arrived at my destination, I sat thinking. *The next time you go out, carry your teeth in your purse until you get where you're going. It's safer.* Especially since I seem to remember, unlike others, I wasn't even embarrassed about the incident.

Shifting Gears

When the decade of the 90's approached, my girlfriends and I kept thinking about how old we were and what we were doing. I thought about it a lot. Is this it? My son becoming a young adult and his mother, me, doing nothing I had dreamed I would do. That's when I decided that a course of action was needed. I obviously wasn't going to be put out to pasture because there were to many more years in my life. It was time to get started. So, I promised myself I would go through a metamorphosis. I had to. My life had more to offer me. More is what I wanted.

Resurrecting my dreams into reality wasn't easy. Hell, life isn't easy at any stage, let alone forty. Sure I knew a little more than I did twenty years earlier, but the wisdom just kept me one step ahead of various calamities. Yet, there was this undying urge to create a new life. Life began at forty is what

I had always heard. I was just a baby and that was my new attitude. Using that sentiment as a beacon to guide me, I was going to follow my heart. I created a five-year plan. My intention? Finish college and obtain that dream degree in journalism, publish a book, and buy a house in the country. If I didn't travel around the world that would be okay, because it's not that important anyway. My imagination would travel for me. I wouldn't waste one minute of thought, because I was going to be a writer. After all of that, who'd know what I would be doing. Getting on in years taught me one thing. Taking one step at a time accomplished more than running a marathon, just ask the tortoise. Besides, I was only going to be forty. I had time.

This brings me back to me and my girlfriends. We all had turned forty by 1993 and went through transformations. Two of us went back to school. One moved out of state and two others just changed jobs. Suddenly, we were all looking forward to being reborn, rejuvenated, and rejoiced. Some say at the age of forty you go through a mid-life crisis, I don't know if that's true. All my girlfriends and I wanted was to evolve into something we thought was greater than we had been. We turned forty. We had no plans on leaving earth then. Maybe adding a little ump in our lives, but not calling it quits. So we were a little older. Our bodies had changed some. We no longer went dancing once a week or stayed up all night on Fridays. Our taste for life had matured. Afternoon tea was pleasing and community activities made us feel productive. What can I say?

I just know that I wasn't what I had been twenty years earlier. None of us were. Over the hill I wasn't either. All I needed was to shift gears. So that's what I did. I moved my life's drive shaft from "D" to "2." Slowed down some and starting heading in a new direction. I bought a house, not the country cottage, but a house. I got the degree and as you can see I finished the book. I did it! Now when I start thinking about turning fifty, I won't fret over it. I'll just shift gears . . . again.

About the Author

Ms. McClain currently writes a weekly column, *The Warrendale Minute: Sylvia Speaks* in the Sunday Press & Guide. She has been featured in the online magazine of Writer's Digest in the Speak Out section. She conducts workshops for writers in money management. The workshops have been conducted at Wayne County Community College and the YWCA. She has been a guest columnist and contributing writer for the Michigan Chronicle, has been quoted in The Detroit Free Press and The Detroit News and has written feature stories published by The University of Michigan-Dearborn in the university's Lyceum. Ms McClain has also done poetry readings in celebration of Black History Month.

Ms. McClain holds a Bachelor of General Studies: Communications, English, and Art History degree from the University of Michigan-Dearborn. She presently serves as a board member of The Detroit Writer's Guild and is responsible for the recording of financial data. Ms. McClain has been on the board of Project Sis (a nonprofit organization for teens at risk) and her other volunteer work has been with WTVS Public TV and Volunteer Income Tax Assistance (VITA).

Ms. McClain is single and has one child. She lives in Detroit.

Need More Copies? Order Direct.

Skipping Through Life, The Reason I Am
by Sylvia McClain

$13.00
ISBN 0-9742643-2-6

Name: _____

Address: _____

_____

City/State/Zip Code: _____

Email: _____

Fax: _____

Cash ☐   Check ☐   Money Order ☐

Include $3.95 for shipping and handling.
Make checks/M.O. payable to: RPM Enterprises

Mail to:
RPM Enterprises
7287 Vaughn
Detroit, MI 48228

Considering Self-Publishing?
Contact **AQUARIUS PRESS** Today!

AQUARIUS PRESS
Humanity Through the Written Word

PO Box 23096
Detroit, MI 48223
(313) 316-0918

aquariuspress@sbcglobal.net
www.aquariuspress.homestead.com
www.buchananenterprises.net

Aquarius Press is a division of H. Buchanan Enterprises.